AS WE ARE SUNG

Christina Mengert

As We Are Sung

Burning Deck/Anyart, Providence

ACKNOWLEDGMENTS:

Some of the poems in this book first appeared in *American Poet, Boston Review, Colorado Review, Copper Nickel, Omnidawn Poetry Blog, Parthenon West Review,* and *Tarpaulin Sky.*

Burning Deck is the literature program of Anyart: Contemporary Arts Center, a tax-exempt (501c3), non-profit organization.

The cover reproduces "Peinture 1993" by Patricia Erbelding (oil, rust, wax, and paper on canvas, 195 x 130 cm).

© 2011 by Christina Mengert
ISBN13: 978-1-886224-05-6, original paperback

Table of Contents

PART A

A Song We Praise as Song	11
Who Can Tell These Things Apart	12
Rest	13
As We Are Sung	14
Gone to Ground	16
Dance as a Metaphor for Thought	17
Confession in Arabesque	18
Echo	19
Flowers on Fire	20
Theatre	21
If Brass Wakes a Bugle	22
First False Start	23
Second False Start	24
Rehearsal	25
Reincarnation of a Lovebird	26
Afterlife	27
Diabolus in Musica	28

BRIDGE

Spectrum	33
Shield & Cloth	35
In Order	36

PART B

And the Morning Stars Sang Together	41
As a Sigh Is	42
There are So Many Rooms in this House	43
Performative	44

Upper Limit Music	45
The Wildness is Interior	46
Manner of Speaking	47
Nectary (A Waltz)	48
Somniloquy (Nocturne)	49
Everybody Hates a Weatherman	50
Quarter Note, Caesura, Quarter Note	51
Ave Maria	52
I've Forgotten How to Speak	53
How to Sing	54
Common Time	56
Cut Time	57
Perfect Time	58
Improvisation	59
Dialogue with Music	60
Biographical Note	63

> *Now*
> *   you sing;*
> *And I, muted,*
> *Yet vibrate—throughout to that*
> *   song's burden*
> *"Spare us—spare us—spare us*
>
> *   From loveliness."*
>
>   Frances Gregg, "To H.D."

> *... since a song does not turn back*
> *   to speak to*
> *Everyone of its order, but will run on*
> *In the words after the sun on*
> *The singer stops shining...*
>
>   Louis Zukofsky, *A*

Part A

A SONG WE PRAISE AS SONG

Where a thing begins or ends —

the knife a ribbon the ribbon a knife

soft-palette strung to remembrance

      "of a certain generality and a certain depth"

      worthy idea — Greek, conveyable

the song that is sung between notes

I've heard him call I've answered

who could tell these things apart?

WHO CAN TELL THESE THINGS APART
for Bin Ramke

Neither song nor

argument, the extension

of the tongue into one's

butterflied body. Rest.

It is an agony. Like leaves

agonize their unfurling

the body agonizes its

changing state. Attempt

(archaically, daggers, spears)

to pierce call pierce

response   an attempt

that is *Musica ficta* —

it is not song but it

is singing.

Rest

each time I think of you, you cease to be
— Jacques Roubaud

A bird, a stone – the body

is overturned. We lay it down

and call it "bolts of cloth." Also

"lands of unlikeness." Like a

phonograph, it is proof

we render the natural to scale,

more than motion, an incantation

brought back to the slick wreath

of human expression. Listen:

the page shudders, yes, like a sea.

Listen: who can hear the rest   (only the rest)

As we are sung

An art of repetitions – which?

*

Your flowers strung these serious flowers strung

I gather buckets – joy! Or grain, more solemn.

*

When in light, bodily   call out what we

see: lapses or shade. Eyes in your lamplight.

*

Elsewhere nothing matches half of midday's

records; we are folded at the center.

*

I am lost in the bell of your (sun
you are
shining, my
shuttering mind
is re-)
dress.

*

Hardening postures of landscape, our

flowers and fields are not novel, but struck.

*

I am too. We. Burnt live things

      outside light: constructed visage sounding

what? A garden. What? A music. What? Return.

Shhh, ah. Shhh, ah. Shhh, ah.

GONE TO GROUND

There is a string
we pull from the earth into
the wailing room

that sound
we set to fire

Dance as a Metaphor for Thought

Thatched flesh of a trumpet – snarled threads
made whole by continuous air – buttress and chain!

I put my lips to it. We agree to an imminence of sound
but what sound? I breathe out. The air shudders away.

*

We accumulate toward a way

of seeing that tomorrow will become
the stuff of jars –

spirit of gravity and collusion

shhh. Forget your fetters and give
the earth a variable host of names.

*

Remind me to feed upon them, as they
have fed upon us. In the beginning, there was
affirmation – yes – yes, the worms were a beautiful
body latched.

A thought: the body that eats the body is dancing.
Long graceful arm of the disappearing world.

Confession in Arabesque

If every tongue and every sign and whatever is subject to transience were wholly stilled

we might find ourselves alive in the position

of arrival.   Call will and emerge —   the nest that suffers for itself

buried   in the convulsive wick of a voice

as how in stillness we find making

or from a distance   lands crash like overlarge birds

Counterpoint:

I've seen hands   buckled into landscape

What fossils, these hands.

Echo

Where the hollowing folds   upon folds

a story goes: a king asks men to fill a room
the answer is light   but if not light
(failing match, wet air, ambitious sun)
a speaking answer   I've heard

a speaking answer   time's unspoken architecture

unrepeatable, unrepeatable

Flowers on Fire

Everything happens in the blue hours
or everything is prepared to happen

Shrieking clarinets, tulips—

*

"I do become things," she said, meaning
inside, like a wick.

Like a bell.

*

What kind of music is made of bows and flesh, bows of flesh? The kind we locate in the star-machine of the inner ear. Listen! The bleating of crescendo.

The field of hollyhocks is burning and all this heat.

*

Of course I've forgiven you. You
seeded the ground and called it
"come alive." It's the old question

of the hollow or the stick. Or is it
the sound alone that fashions
itself– anticipation, resistance,

a dry, dry day.

Theatre

Call the resembling body, "cinematic evacuation."

Ambulant fossil. Here, again, the thunder of
performance. Against the aisle, what makes

a fog of what holds this thunder to our ears.

*

Do you remember (conversion)
pushing sound out black bars – it was a sad effort

the weight of it sadly diminished

*

Later I fix the problem. *The true miracle was walking on mirrors.* Now this:
we've broken open the hard shell, loosed into the excitement of the storm.

*

What, then, do you mean by resembling?
Arrested, visible thing. Catch it up
in air we conjure from the deepest-most parts.

It isn't right, I know, leaving like this,
the mirrors having gotten us this far.

If Brass Wakes a Bugle

We find silence to be the discipline of sound.

A severed ear conducts its own silence, or what does he say?

That the instrument blames its material seems true enough, or the body announces its waking with blustering sound.

Spectator, the ear in your hand is trying to listen.

It's a question of making and of limit. Finite instrument against infinite (measured to be greater than): string, rosewood, hollow, violin, violins, gust and sound.

Yes, we call the frame a distinguishing act of creation. Meanwhile, crows in the distance crowing a death song

drawn into some other town.

First False Start

This is a rehearsal
for the end. All these years
building up bones, blues
and clovers, all
excuses in the miniature
name of awe.

Second false start

Again: the end
rehearses. It needs props –
plastic trees, scaffolding,
an apparatus for flying.

Play it again. Play
the song again. You
know what I want
to hear.

Rehearsal

Paper birds regard
this room as if
it were a true space.

We regard the paper
way they mean to fly.

I've seen the way
your thoughts, some
nights, are ashamed.

The way, modernly,
flesh turns on like a light.

How it asks
everything and demands
everything.

I've seen
this performance   before—

Your piano is out of tune.
Or it was. Keep
your head down
when you bow.

Reincarnation of a Lovebird

> *And so they are ever returning to us, the dead.*
> — W. G. Sebald

Tonight you are on trial.
You are wearing the night-
dress of available skin.

You recount a thousand kisses.
This takes time.

In the later hours, the tonic
is applied like a salve.

The public admires.

"It's not like staying at home,
I can tell you that."

Movement throws your figure
into relief. Ironic — remembering
how a thing touched

is indistinguishable
from a thing touching —

So you are crime and verdict.

AFTERLIFE

Half-life
over & over

oh, oh —

There is no
silence that is not
kinetic.

A boat on its way
to bridge;

you'd think we'd
have forgotten
by now

what it feels like
to transgress.

Applause! Applause!

Rest.

Funny valentine
my funny valentine.

Diabolus in Musica

Sprechstimme. The body cannot be a church as an architecture cannot be a grove or saturation cannot be this entire painting. Here is a chord. From here to there to there.

Or the body is a meeting place but what is its business? I'm writing you with my voice. These letters rise and fall as a method of intent and failure.

It is the organ growing itself wrongly, growing bulk. A stranger's fugue of the body. It sounds like the world melting. Humming.

A thousand years ago I called you in just the same way. You said I was rotting from the inside and I said no, the note is flat. And you said, as I said. And I left weeping.

The instrument is an example of hands pressing ecstatically into the world. Glenn Gould sings back to its singing. So does Charles Mingus and everyone.

What does it mean to have a necessary relation to the world? Simply to be in it, entering like a juggler of wild cats, a performer of alternating consequence and inconsequence.

If an act extends beyond its termination (Hazlitt!), do we suffer its ecstasy forever? Do we gather its strings and blow into its mouthpiece? Do we spend ourselves in unanswerable questions?

Ti mi dadum. When the left hand rests, it is either patience or desperation. Outside, where everything receives, birds make their own noise. Oh Colliding Parts! Oh Polyphony!

This is what we learn in any given moment – the difference between unity and coherence (hear, here), what breaks apart as we stand at the window, in our bathrobes, pulling music

from instrument to the ear pressed to a hollow infant we shrink to when quiet. If it shrieks, we are shrieking. And if it murmurs, we are writing a poem.

Bridge
(DEFINITIONS)

SPECTRUM

> *How many traits*
> *must a thing have*
> *in order to be singular?*
> — Rae Armantrout

1.

Blood and ember
flowers of various lightning
rose, poppy, a certain iris
of soil or earth
clay hands
dust about the legs
like falling, swung material
observe: a dedicated blush
at the sudden attention
of human weather
bursting from its ripe
ripe skins

2.

said of distant hills, thin milk, undraped sky
we agree to say it, to point and say it
on the other side of burning on the other
side of blood, what we know to be the absence
of weather, held or trapped breath
sad, unchanging, the sound of a note
orbiting badly the planet of its mood

my mouth is a brush
tongue flicked at these

3.

most luminous
embryos, are you
afraid? we have
taken you to the sun
not to burn but to
sicken, how events
just recorded sicken
with time the event
of your death bright
and I, like a cat
swallowing a canary
alerted by song
but dimly, a quiet song

SHIELD & CLOTH

Every word was once a poem.
— Ralph Waldo Emerson

1.

I go like a lamb.

Freezing, tender page
or shuddering: behold
a pale: how return becomes
what's there.

2.

Literal or not, it's taken on
too much! exhausted light,
the wickedness of exhausted
eyes. Grief dons a bruise
and scares; the soaked
scarring of assignation. Call it
what you will, want: no
number of rabbits will
ever make one of these horses.

IN ORDER

FIRST

That is before or is
seed, preceding days
the idea of days what
comes that we don't
see except by touching
the space between here
and there before gone
in the chivalric sense
of mare and bended knee,
what we don't believe
like centaurs, clocks
when there is nothing
under the sun or nothing
that suspends for this long.

NEXT

That is the geography
of pursuit – sought in
the night of what I am
beside you, the ivy of
days and of body, Lady
double-backed & beckoning.

We hunt our shadows
for the realization of
position, vague meat
I bring to the table but
do not eat.

LAST

Whence in immaterial sense
a trace, furrow that is
the beginning and end
to plow through the face
with a wooden foot. Yes,
set your brains upon it,
let the cobbler stick to
what the cobbler sticks to.
Find it simple, cardinal,
as kisses or hawks
artfully measured
and found to be late
but not least. And of
this age and blame,
a thing dwells and you
endure, a waterman
like to an amateur.

Part B

And the Morning Stars Sang Together

> *What is a Nightmare? Is it a Kind of Horse?*
> — H.D.

Said the twig to the flower, the flower to the twig –
a sound, paint spread over a raincoat, happy trembling lovers.

"I desire my dust to be mingled with yours"

for a time – reserved hours (like wanting) blinked into form.

"But you are iron" – lightning rose up, the living

birds scattered. Nevermind, nevermind,

is it a nest? Is it a kind of mind? The sweet-bitter

and wildness of two and two: lilies, lily-pads, laurels, branches

The way to know a thing, she said, is by the catalogue
that succeeds it.

                                      Slowly, in frames
              look over: a rose.

                        A sea rose? See: there is
no wind under water. The petals' fabric in stalled swish.

"Not roses at all, not orange blossoms even"

Nor rain, nor raincoats, the absorbed body shot through

with stiff earth. One ear turned to hear what calls
birdlike, accurate: rose, rose, rose,

As a Sigh Is

> *I am an organ that breathes, and through breathing
> comes closer and closer to speech.*
> — Kristin Prevallet

A chink on the inside of sound.
Or a way that breath means (of itself, probably a ghost).

        Yes, all bodies are haunted, air
against enclosure, the metal skins or wood and reed of the tongue.
All bodies are haunted. And the world? A whisper, I think,
without a mouth. And the world? A camel, busses, a rooftop

(on fire!), a hat stand, a sentence: at the top and bottom of everything,
a sound the body persuades

        like a telephone—

"I am here."

"I am a comical bird – hieroglyph of bird soul"

"And you?"

"And you?"

There are so many rooms in this house

In a dream I heard him say "egrets"

but as a verb, as in "sound egrets through space"

a mild soaring

*

In another dream, he corrects himself: what I mean to say

is *egress,*

pretty abandon

*

Some nights we recognize the latch in our hands
as something simple, like a daisy

other nights it is the reason we fail to love
or organize sound into the meat of our failure.

*

To hear yourself dreaming in someone else's
mouth – that is, a mind (your own, others) brought

to bear in blind, quiet garden. Lay here. Listen.
The throat of your voice on wings.

Performative

> *There must exist an accepted conventional procedure having a certain conventional effect, the procedure to include the uttering of certain words by certain persons in certain circumstances.*
> — J.L. Austin

I sing. No. *I sing.*
Le mot just or the just note.

Wandering from here
the book opens onto a river and the river says, "we make measures
to compensate for memory" — i.e., recapitulation.

And for what the coda? A writer says,

"in such and such story, I write a character who wears a hat
always: in the shower, making love, walking a tightrope."

It is operatic because it is baffling. Anything can wear a hat.

Like a bell— the book is vibrational; it learns the air.

How agreeable the invisible.

UPPER LIMIT MUSIC

Say Ah. Now sing it.

Between speech and song: a grace note

air, airs (think, now sing!)

wind burnt into weather—

Words turned hedonistic, like I touch you
and arch. Like ah. A parasite.

Charming. Then sad. Then charming.

The edge resembles many things but mostly
hymen. God of the brink. O Hymen, Hymenaios,

for whose bed do we breathe lightning?
                                                I believe

you are coming –

(pipes, animate silence   ah, ah, thump!)

The thing about voice? No where
is it not a poem.

The Wildness Is Interior

for Dottie Lasky and Gaston Bachelard

That music is fled; our reaction
to daydreaming is to call color out
and also expectation. The music
is a nest but not a shell and these
things are different as one red lip
to another red lip. I ask you what
you are looking at and you say,
"sometimes your breasts, sometimes
the fire" and I think this must be
what is called the aesthetics of shiny
things, like how birds fall headlong
into the hard earth and only then
look back into the hidden places
for import and understanding. You took
my picture several times but not
just my picture, always with new light,
angle, recording the awkward expression
of the watched. If only I could daydream
before cameras, or all the music in the world
comes and goes in the form of longing
so I can say, "sound is a forward presentation"
even as the space is rounding to make
everything available, though really
it always was, buried in my body
like risky pearls.

Manner of Speaking

It is imaginary: a bone, color,
shelves of sound – like rocks

through which snakes and light

put the voice to measure

and within measure, a pause
that looks like a gap. Again.

Shhh and shhh.

Put your *glissando* back in its hat.

Hello melody.

Nectary (a Waltz)

Put the bird in a box.
Flutter, flutter, flutter.

The box spins. A down beat.
Something bursts the inside.

As the natural appears
crooked, various, sown

(bees and their one long note)
the unnatural straightens.

A symphony! Sonata!
Art of imposed order.

Like a garden of song
the clock ticks (yards and yards).

What sudden expression
of flower parts, quaking.

Last marvel before seed —
all the life in and in

lips, tongue, teeth it is no
wonder you grow outside.

Somniloquy (Nocturne)

When you say, threshold,

      no, when you say
go back to the beginning

I believe you prophet.

(In the sleeping place speech
is a kind of harmony — else,
semitone)

Even this has rhythm

even the sleeping deaf
and tongues, adjusted
like halos over inside quiet.

            I speak into the half-heart
of your ear. It evaporates —

         as all things that open seem
         as elsewhere, as here.

Everybody Hates a Weatherman

About the rain— it seems
uncertain

unlike the way we feel
the rest of the world
as applied pressure

(not the obvious tactility of putting your hand out and rough, smooth, various
combinations, flimsy as insect wings depending on the insect, brittle, mostly
shard)

When I speak into your ear
it is like rain –

and I wonder if it is so
simple as my thought
becomes your thought

or if there is a
median voice— screen
or front of weather

(bonjour, barometer)

that says, "her voice
is a pelican's voice,

how sad, how sad."

Open your humid
mouth and see

Caesura

It may be open — the way *muse*
is open-mouthed but dancing. Feet

feet and rhythm!

Harmony is late.

Is it leaping?

The days you take me to sit
and listen the down of small
animals in our ears we shake
and shake. Silly chicks.

Unrest gets thick. We slip
inside and wiggle. Tape our
jaws to take in *something running*.

Startle response: little pulse

made exuberant. Or sudden wonder

and hush. Un-stopped.

Ave Maria

for Maria Callas

    I know
your name by ecstasy of song
only; in the plastic space of
delay, crescendo, the spastic pliés
of a meaningful column of air.
It is hot outside and the birds
wriggle your body; a mouth you open
to return heights to those who
would have them.

It is a kind of reverberation,
the birds gathering distance
in the folds of your wet wings.

I'VE FORGOTTEN HOW TO SPEAK

I do think about the sensation; sun lodged
on the inside, sky peeling itself under skin.

He says, "do not mistake… a waterfall for a harbor."

So much for calling out the interior.
So much for fishermen in the dark.

How to Sing

Having never met you, I can only imagine
the purple fringe of your shirt, how I will
sit and ask silly questions: how elemental
is elemental, do you like Mozart and/or

to dance? Finally, the world shifts to bare
its bare shoulders, soft belly, the planet
underneath the planet. We breathe. It is
a necessary first step. What I want, today,

is a flute, mini-piano, to take the edge off
— I mean, how naked the hours
feel open to whatever song folds you into
its glass gown. *Blue now,* while the skin

of sound snakes through the grass we
get down in. Swings and rises. I imagine
lifting through eyes, masks, opening
the easy chest of dark, dark pulling

like thunder (a body that is the mind's
weather). I imagine your quiet, my
comical performance of conjuring
balloons in shapes, moon-walk, any

one thing that keeps the nude mouth
unexpected — it is so inside-out, what
we do here. The sad irony of
hidden things. So, here, I look for you:

were you my audience or was I yours?
And this, skin. And this, muscle. And
this, bone. Underneath, that space your
hands plunge through — that: *to sing*.

Common Time

Discriminate ear — what can't
you hear if you have time?

The whole of sound, like
the whole of thought   we step into

and out of; it changes

or we change. A squeaky brake, wind
through a tunnel, always airplanes —

Is it a record
or a bad child we take a baton to?

Tap, tap, tap, tap. What love
resists evolution; what
evolution resists agreement —

I see you cutting wheat in a gone field.
It is everything at once and you are
well, a thing forgot to listen.

CUT TIME

A run:
Lift-off origin.

Virtuoso your hat
is on fire.

Perfect Time

What does not involve you,
bewildered mind — or this
process of translation?

If I had an orchard or saints,
or a way of being always
dead and living — go on, go on.

The value of a note underlying
earth, root, mantle, core: such
a thing you breathe yourself into

and fold into explicable laundry.
Take the orange tree. What does
it know? This signature punch-line.

IMPROVISATION

I like to think of sound as a formal site of resistance.

Put away your flourishes. What year is this?

It is the year of one foot after the other and go.

It is the year you take off your hat and sing Gilbert & Sullivan.

Or something between you and it is ecstasy.

Where the animals and trumpets yawp a grassy knoll.

No, not that kind. The other kind.

Honk your horn if you love this orchestra.

I mean, honk your horn if you have a horn to honk.

Heave, ho. It's a wonder a man could keep up a whistle.

Time, time. Check the schedule. We're taking the world with us
                                            when we go.

Dialogue with Music

after Paul Fattaruso

The closet of music is filled with bowler hats, dresses (gingham, sequined), poodle-skirts, vests, cuff-links.

The music takes you to dinner, pulls out your chair, orders the veal.

You thank the music. You wonder, is anything really that polite?

The music strips you and bends you over. The bed of music

is only sheets. Silk, cotton, flannel, sheepskin — sheets upon sheets.

The kitchen of music is all brass and no tile.

Music denies the encounter. It argues its own impossible nature.

The argument of music is bodiless attention. You bent yourself over.

Music was simply the occasion for bending. You remind the music

it was once a thing for nighttime and learning. It reminds you

that the use of a thing is not the thing but the thing in hands.

You think about that. The music waits.

You sometimes forget about music. Like other things, music doesn't mind.

It is above your noticing. That is, above this notation.

Music, it says, is the thing that fills the spaces between matter. It adds,

"and God." You think about this, and ask music if it or God has need

of the human ear. It positions itself at the peak of a mountain, crosses

its legs, and says: *if a tree falls in a forest, and all the ears of the forest*

have fallen like acorns to the ground, there is no sound but waves shuddering through the world. So no? You ask. Music closes its eyes. Music is difficult to understand.

You ask many things of music though it asks nothing of you.
Most days, music is nowhere to be found. It feels old-fashioned,
and requests an invitation. You bend over. It accepts.
You and music meet in the middle. There are sirens and chimes.
Your body is a fermata over the small point of music.
Afterward, the room stills. There is nothing to be said
when music comes. The ecstasy of music is like many colored
paper folded into the shape of a bird. You curl into the bodiless
abstraction and pretend an instrument. Music will seem indifferent
and sneak out while you sleep. You bury yourself
in the bed that smells of music, and weep, and exalt. How
many nights have you been filled with music! Outside,
the world begins to rain. The tiny ears of the earth quiver
and accept. It is the witness of music as music is your
witness. The threads of the sky turn your breath to sound.
You spit into the mouth of music and it spits back. It is
the ancient way of lovers.

BIOGRAPHICAL NOTE

Christina Mengert has crossed the country from her native Georgia via Rhode Island to Denver (where she earned a Ph.D. in English/Creative Writing) and now on to New York State, to teach in Bard College's Prison Initiative Program.

She is co-editor of *12x12: Conversations in 21st century Poetry and Poetics* (University of Iowa Press). Her poems have appeared in *Aufgabe, Colorado Review, Copper Nickel, Parthenon West Review, The New Review of Literature, Web Conjunctions*, etc., her reviews in *Colorado Review, Denver Quarterly, Reconfigurations,* and *Constant Critic.*

As We Are Sung is her first book.

This book was designed and computer typeset by Rosmarie Waldrop in 10 pt. Palatino, with Benquiat Frisky initials. Printed on 55 lb. Writers' Natural (an acid-free paper), smyth-sewn and glued into paper covers by McNaughton & Gunn in Saline, Michigan. There are 750 copies.